CANDLE BURNING

An essentially practical explanation of a simple but effective magical art. Includes candle burning rituals for opening psychic perception, expurgating disease, gaining love and happiness. With details of a 'mystical novena' for enlisting aid from the angelic hierarchy in mundane activities.

CANDLE BURNING

Its Occult Significance

by
MICHAEL HOWARD

THE AQUARIAN PRESS
Wellingborough, Northamptonshire

First published 1975
Second edition, revised, enlarged and reset, 1980
Second Impression 1982
Third Impression 1984
Fourth Impression 1986

ISBN 0 85030 168 8 (UK)
ISBN 0 87728 490 5 (USA)

Printed and bound in Great Britain by
Richard Clay (The Chaucer Press) Limited,
Bungay, Suffolk.

CONTENTS

CHAPTER ONE

WHAT IS CANDLE MAGIC?

Since very early times candles have been a source of light and a symbol of comfort to man. Because of their prime importance in day-to-day living candles became surrounded by myths and legends, a fact which illustrates how highly they were regarded.

Imagine, if you can, the scene in a prehistoric cave. Dank, dark and inhospitable. Man had discovered fire but soon realized that its use in a confined space as a source of light was limited. So, in place of fire, he used animal fat to produce a glimmering light which would drive away the night demons. The candle had been created.

Symbolically light has always represented the power of good to man. In the ancient Mysteries of classical times it symbolized wisdom, enlightenment, knowledge and spiritual attainment. By way of contrast darkness meant ignorance, stupidity, evil and the downward descent into materialism. Indeed, every man was believed to contain within his inner self a spark of divine light which could – by correct conduct in the moral sphere – be fanned into a burning flame of great spirituality.

In this way the immortal soul of man was likened to the flame of a candle wavering in the darkness of the world. A gentle breeze could quench his pathetic light yet, in the stillness and tranquillity, the flame rose up defiant and strong. Just as in life, even amid all the troubles and turmoils, the spirit of men defied onslaught from the threatening powers of darkness.

From sublime beliefs such as these arose the practice of candle burning as a magical art. Today, we tend to be rather wary of the word 'magic' and this is mainly due to the centuries of persecution which have rendered the word meaningless to many people. Some equate it with conjurers' tricks or confuse it with devilish pacts and other nonsense. In fact the word 'magic' comes from the root 'magi' which means simply 'wise ones' and refers to an ancient caste of priest magicians from Persia. A magician is merely a wise man skilled in occult (or hidden) arts of nature which are not known or recognized by the majority of his fellows.

Simple Magical Art

Candle burning is the most simple magical art because it employs little ritual, few ceremonial artifacts, and a mode of language easily understandable by everyone. In candle magic the student is never asked to learn the 365 names of God, master such ancient tongues as Hebrew or Sanscrit or dig up mandrakes at the full moon. The 'props' of candle burning can be bought at any department store and its procedures can be performed in any living-room or bedroom in the land. Even in the old days, when magic was almost exclusively the province of the aged scholar who could read and write, candle magic remained the natural occult art practised by ordinary people. Burning candles for magical reasons is not difficult yet it can be said, without much fear of any contradiction, that it is just as potent in action as the words of evocation, triple circles and pentagrams of the magus who practises the 'High Art of Magic'. A lesson which still has to be learnt by many people is that occultism is basically a simple subject made complicated by ignorance and stupidity.

Most of us have already performed our first act of candle magic by the time we are three years old. Remember those early birthdays? Blowing out the candles on top of the cake and making a wish? This custom of childhood is based upon two very important magical principles; concentration and the use of a focusing symbol. In simple terms this means that if you want something to happen you must first concentrate (blow out the candles) and then associate your magical desire (the wish) with the symbolic act of candle snuffing. Your willpower makes the dream come true. Similar techniques are used in magic and the art of candle burning.

Unlike many forms of 'High Magic' one does not need to hold any particular religious belief to practise candle burning. One can be a Sikh, Christian, Buddhist, Moslem, Hindu, Jew, pagan, or none of these, because in candle burning you use your own willpower, desire and the power of your mind to cause results to occur. A belief in a Supreme Creator is, however, requisite and I would presume that everyone who reads this book at least places credence in such an entity. Without this faith any approach towards occultism and psychic matters is rendered null and void.

Perhaps it would be prudent to add that this does not mean that you cannot categorically employ ritual and/or prayers from any religion in candle magic. As we progress into the subject and I begin to give practical spells for the reader to perform it could be said that my approach becomes 'religious' in the sense that the reader finds himself invoking angelic beings. In this book I have referred to the 'angels' because they fit in with my own personal cosmology but the reader is free to interpret these images in terms of his own beliefs. He may regard them as pagan gods, personifications of natural forces, saints, aspects of his own psyche or whatever. If he feels so inclined he can dismiss them entirely, call directly upon the Life Force, God or nothing at all. In fact, the concept of the angelic hierarchy corresponds with all these different images and are merely focusing symbols for the student to concentrate on and identify with during the rite. As stated before, the key to practical burning is *concentration* and it is ultimately the mind of the practitioner which does the work.

Anyone who burns a candle for magical reasons is seeking to liberate and use the subconscious mind. It is one of the foundation stones of occultism that the mind is divided into three distinctive levels; the Conscious, the Subconscious and the Superconscious.

Underworld of the Subconscious
Under normal circumstances the conscious mind

is active during waking hours and is in control of
the body functions and actions of the individual.
During sleep the subconscious mind takes over as
the body relaxes and the conscious mind is
refreshed. This period of mental activity is
usually characterized by dreams, visions and
sometimes nightmares. All these rise up from the
underworld of the subconscious where lurk all
the many atavistic images of our animal nature.
At all times – waking or sleeping – the
superconscious is active keeping the two other
aspects of mind integrated and synchronized.
Although we are aware of both the subconscious
and the conscious aspects it is seldom that man
encounters 'face to face' the superconscious mind
or higher self.

When magic is practised the principal aim of
the magus is to sidetrack the conscious mind –
which is conditioned with preconceived ideas and
limited by conventional personality patterns –
and contact the subconscious, which reacts, not
to words that the subconscious is a very powerful
agent which, when released from captivity and
controlled, can cause changes in environmental
patterns. It is the level of psychic 'feeling' and
telepathy and once liberated it can act as a magic
genie of the lamp, attracting towards its master
the things he desires in life. If misused or abused
however, it can wreak a horrific vengeance by
returning to its master and destroying him.

Some occultists by-pass the subconscious mind
altogether and seek to make contact with the
higher self or, as it is called in old occult books,
'the holy guardian angel'. Not everyone sets their

sights that high and in this section of the book we are concerned only with contacting the subconscious mind. By doing this the practitioner of candle burning can bring into manifestation his desires and wishes, gain the love of others, heal the sick, secure financial aid and progress along the path towards psychic and spiritual attainment.

A word of warning might be prudent at this stage. Like all instruments of occult forces, magic is a two-edged sword. Use it for the wrong purpose and the results of your misdemeanours will rebound back on you. Their effect in reverse is many times greater than the original impetus which sent them on their way. This fact is recognized in the old saying about curses returning threefold to the sender. People who play about with the occult or magic usually burn their fingers before learning to take the subject seriously. A lesson learnt that way may be a cruel one but at least it leaves an impression which is unlikely to be forgotten by the foolish tyro.

In this practical guide to candle burning I have excluded any rituals, spells or procedure likely to cause such harm to my readers. My confidence in their intelligence, good sense and basic moral principles, leads me to believe that they will have no wish to pursue candle magic for purely immoral or evil purposes.

CHAPTER TWO

PREPARING YOUR MAGIC

What kind of candles are used for magical purposes? Size and shape are not really that important. Most practitioners try to regulate their candles to one standard size and type if possible. It makes life a lot simpler and that is what magic is all about. If you follow the example of the experts you will not go wrong.

Magical books lay great stress on 'newness' and one often reads of the magus wearing a robe of *virgin* wool or writing out spells on *virgin* parchment. Likewise, in candle magic, the actual candles used must be brand new and should not have been used for any other purpose. Never, for instance, use a candle which has already been lit on a dinner table or been used as a nightlight. There is a very good occult reason for this insistence on the virginity of material used for magical purposes and that is that the vibrations picked up from other sources will negate the effect of the object in the act of magic.

Some students make their own candles and this is a very useful exercise, for not only does it impregnate the candle with the personal vibrations of the user but in the act of making the candle the student ensouls the wax with his thoughts and desires. Candle making is not as difficult as you may think and many craft or art

shops sell the wax and moulds which you need
for this activity. The hot wax (heated at 180°F
82°C) is poured into a suitable mould, through
which a wick has been threaded, and then left to
solidify by cooling. Perfume or dye can be added
to the wax in the heating process and when the
wax is cooled the mould is removed leaving a
fully formed candle. This sounds an over-
simplification of the process but in fact that is
basically all there is to it. Not only is this extra
effort worth it from a magic point of view, but if
developed, candle making can evolve into a very
profitable hobby.

Having now obtained your candles the next
step is to establish where you are going to do
your magic. One does not need an elaborate
temple – unless you have one already – and any
ordinary room is adequate for the purpose.

Silence is Essential

One thing is essential and that is silence. Candle
magic requires concentration and you cannot
concentrate with background noise impinging on
your thoughts. Also make sure that the room is
well ventilated and is neither too cold nor too hot.
These may seem rather silly precautions but if
you have to spend an hour or more doing your
occult work a certain degree of comfort is
necessary if you are to achieve good results. I do
not subscribe to the 'fasting and flogging' school
of thought which ordains that in order to achieve
anything in the occult sense you must first
subject yourself to torture and physical
discomfort. Such unnatural practices have

nothing to do with genuine occultism.

Clothing is also not too important providing what you wear is loose fitting, clean and comfortable. Some occultists prefer to wear ritual robes, which are symbolic of 'cutting off' from the outside world. Others work nude but personally the thought of hot wax spluttering everywhere has made me always keep my clothes on!

Incense can also be burnt during candle burning to help provide a suitable 'occult' atmosphere and to act as an agent to stimulate the mental and psychic senses. You can combine incense and candles by buying or making wax candles to which perfume or incense grains have been added. In my opinion incense is not an essential part of candle burning but is a nice smell to have around anyway.

One of the most important stages of candle burning is 'oiling' or 'dressing' the candle. A reason for this rather peculiar practice is rather difficult to discover but since it has been an integral part of candle burning for centuries few practitioners question its validity. (In some ways this is wrong because if there is no logical reason for a magical act then, providing lapsing from its practice does not affect the end results, there would seem to be little reason for continuing the outmoded action.)

In this case it would seem that the idea of oiling the candle is to forge a psychic link between it and the magus by means of that important sensory experience, touch. Only by touching does the developing baby learn at an early age to relate to and understand the outside world. By physically oiling the candle you are passing in to the candle, through your hands, your own vibrations and making the candle an extension of the powers of your mind.

For the purpose of oiling the candle is regarded as a psychic magnet having a 'north pole, and a 'south pole'. When anointing the candle with oil the practitioner rubs the liquid into the wax commencing at the top or north pole and works downwards to the halfway point. All the time the oil is brushed in a down direction. This process is then repeated in reverse beginning at the south pole and working upwards to the middle of the candle.

As candle burning has become a very neglected art in this country the student has to rely on natural oils or perfumes to complete this 'dressing' procedure. Some occult suppliers will sell you special candle oils with exotic names. Most of these concoctions are totally worthless and the genuine candle burner is advised to shun them and use his own common sense and inventiveness in obtaining his range of oils.

While you oil the candle focus your mind on the purpose you have in view. Concentrate on the reasons for oiling the candle, try to visualize your dream coming true, your wish granted and your desire accomplished. By doing all this you are unconsciously (subconsciously) projecting your thoughts into the ether and thoughts have wings and are living entities. By building up an astral image of what you want you are laying out the blueprint of the reality which will come about by your daydreaming.

Projected Thought Form

Every architect's dream house, every writer's bestseller and every painter's 'Old Master' was first conceived in the imagination, in the mind of the artist. Thus, every completed act, every attained result of magical working is first practised and finalized in the mind of the magus. The ritual actions which follow are designed to act as solidifying agents to make concrete a projected thought form sent from the mind of the candle burner. In essence the ritual acts as the power thrust which brings the thought from imagined completion to physical manifestation on the material plane.

The person who takes up practical candle magic is not asked to deprive the body of the essentials of life. However, it may be found that temporary abstaining from heavy, spicy food a few hours before a rite could be of benefit to the end results. As well as this, a ban on sex for twenty-four hours before the burning of the candles helps to 'charge up' the psychic batteries, which are depleted by love making. Usually the magician will take a bath before commencing the ritual for symbolically he is washing away the negative thoughts of the mind as well as the dirt from his body. On another level he is cleansing the aura of impurities.

CHAPTER THREE

ASTRAL COLOURS
AND ASTROLOGICAL SIGILS

Having prepared both the candles and ourselves, the next step is to decide for what purpose we are going to work magic. It is supposed to be an old rule of occultism that you should never work magic or use occult forces to help yourself in any way. In my experience this adage is now archaic. The reasoning today is, quite rightly, that although the aim of occultism is 'to know in order to serve', how can you help others if you are not in a position to offer help?

To use a bad simile – one beggar is not much help to another beggar. Both are in identical predicaments, both face the same obstacles without posessing the weapons to fight these odds. However, if one beggar decides to better himself then he can rise out of the gutter and – when he is established in life – return to aid his former colleague. Not, of course, by giving him a free hand out but by assisting him to follow his example and rise up to overcome the difficulties of his pitiful existence.

I realize this may seem a crude example to use but the object of all forms of practical occultism, including candle burning, is to make everyone equal and the symbolic 'beggars' in our midst redundant. The theme of those occult schools who say that magic should not be used to better one seems to be to bring everyone down to the level of wanderers in the gutters of life. All men will be equal but only equal as beggars. Such policies merely encourage the lazy to become lazier and prey on the hard working, causing them to seek unlimited help from 'do-gooders' rather than progressing themselves on the Path.

Candle burning can be performed for a number of different purposes, ranging from overcoming bad habits, attracting love or money, settling disturbed atmospheres, protecting against negative forces, regaining lost health, developing psychic powers, and so on. You can see by this short list, which could be expanded upon, that not all these requests are 'selfish' ones and anything you ask for yourself can be asked for a third person by inserting their name at the correct stage in the rite.

Colour a Powerful Medium

One of the most important requisites in candle burning is the actual colour of the candle. Colour is a very powerful medium. We speak of people suffering from 'the blues', being in a 'black mood' or having a 'flaming row'. All these common expressions refer to colours and link them with the emotions and desires of man. They are used to isolate and describe certain psychological reactions of happiness, joy and good humour or misery, anger and depression.

Colours are shades of light vibrating at different rates. Red and black may vibrate slower than white or blue so they register on our optical nerves as 'darker' shades of light and because of this they cause different reactions in the viewer. Tests in hospitals prove that patients recover faster in wards painted green or blue than in rooms decorated in dull colours like grey and brown. We are far happier on sunny days when the predominant colour scale is blue/green than on cloudy days when grey/black/brown are in evidence.

Because of the different effects of colour on the human psyche and the environment, different coloured candles are used for varying magical purposes. For the reader's guidance I have listed below the main colours of the spectrum and their meanings.

WHITE represents purity, spirituality and the higher attainments of life which can be achieved by the developed man.

RED symbolizes health, energy, strength, sexual potency and courage.

PINK is the colour of love, affection and all the exalted virtues of romance.

YELLOW is intellect, imagination, the power of the mind. It is very symbolic of creativity, the artist, also charm, confidence and gentle persuasion.

GREEN equals abundance and fertility. It is the colour of luck, good fortune and generosity.

BLUE means truth, inspiration, wisdom, occult power and protection. It is the colour of understanding and good health.

PURPLE represents success in finance and the stock market. Psychic ability of a higher type, power, idealism and self-dignity.

GOLD attracts higher influences, while

SILVER removes negative powers and opens the gates to the astral plane.

As each colour relates to a psychic note, so also does it relate to the signs of the zodiac, for astrology can be an important factor in candle burning through its links with the planetary angels. If the working you are doing concerns two people – perhaps yourself and a friend – then it might be useful to discover the birth signs under which the two individuals were born. Candles of the correct zodiacal colour can then be used in the working to represent the people who are involved.

Example of Typical Spell

In order to illustrate this and also to present a typical format for a candle burning spell, I have formulated the following hypothetical example:

Let us imagine that Mr A is in love with Miss B and that she does not return his affection. A decides to petition the 'powers-that-be' through candle burning to attract Miss B's love. He first acquires three new candles. For the sake of our experiment, let us say that A is a Gemini (21 May-20 June) and that Miss B is a Libran (23 September-22 October). He would therefore select a yellow candle to represent himself and a blue candle to symbolize Miss B. The third candle in the trinity would be pink, which is the colour of exalted love.

A sets the three candles in a triangle, making sure that the blue and yellow ones are six inches apart and that the pink candle is near to them.

This working is performed on a Friday, a day sacred to the goddess of love, and when the moon is waxing. Because love is the subject of the working, A will put his petition to the angel Anael who has rulership over affairs of the heart.

The two candles representing the lovers are lit and A says:

'As I light these two flames I imagine B's heart burning with love for me as mine does for her. I see her body consumed by the flames of pure love and her eyes aglow with desire. Together we are united in the sacred bond of love, understanding and ecstasy.'

He then visualizes Miss B and thinks of the great happiness they would have together, laughing, happy, at one with each other and the big, wide world about them.

A petitions the angel Anael thus:

'Anael, Angel of Venus! Melt B's heart with the overflowing love of all creation. Let her see me as I really am. Cast aside from her eyes the mists of illusion. If she really thinks anything of me let her come to me and unite in love everlasting.'

He then draws upon a sheet of clean paper a 'diagram of intent', containing cryptic symbols relating to the matter worked. In this instance two entwined hearts with the names of the lovers underneath would suffice. The paper is folded up and burnt in the candle flames and A then moves the yellow and blue candles forward till they touch. Then the three lights are left to burn down.

Basic Elements of Candle Lore

Certain basic elements of candle lore are contained within this little working. Firstly, the use of different coloured candles to represent the petitioned matters and the people involved. Secondly, the use of a day connected with the matter (Friday) and the invoking of the angel or god ruling the matter (Anael). Thirdly, the recital of intent, the concentration, visualization and symbolic act of binding (burning the sigil and moving the candles). Lastly, the performance of the working when the moon was waxing.

In all types of magic the phases of the moon are important. When the moon is waxing (increasing towards full) then you attract beneficial conditions to you. When it is waning (decreasing towards the new moon) you banish negative conditions from your surroundings. It is true the moon only reflects the rays of the sun but it does so in a way which causes certain degrees of magnetic polarization to occur. Psychic power ebbs and flows with the moon tides and a wise man follows these tides in magic.

CHAPTER FOUR

SPELLS FOR
GAIN, LOVE AND HAPPINESS

Candle burning is a form of magic sometimes referred to as 'elemental', which means that it is connected with one of the four elements; air, water, fire and earth. As one would easily guess, candle burning comes under the rulership of the element of fire. Because of this it has as its patron the Archangel Mikael or Michael, who is Lord of the Sun.

Before doing candle magic at all it might be advisable to align yourself with the occult ray of the Archangel Michael, for as the old saying says: 'the Gods are excellent friends but terrible enemies.' As Michael rules fire he also has dominion over the 'salamanders', or elemental spirits of the flame, who are in turn ruled by an elemental king, Djinn. These fire spirits can aid your workings but like all denizens of the elemental kingdoms, they can cause plenty of trouble if upset.

Petition to the Archangel Michael
To avoid such unfortunate incidents I would suggest that you petition the protection and aid of the solar angel.

O Angel Michael, Lord Protector and Archangel of the Sun, aid me in my magical work. Guide me along the true Path that my steps may never falter along that well-trod way. Lend thy power to my efforts as I mould the flames of thy element into creative impulses controlled by my will.

Then, addressing the elemental king of fire:

O Djinn, Lord of Flame! I ask thy help and the help of thy spirits in the magical work. Strengthen my will, increase my power and burn deep with the astral light the desires which I unleash. Do this, O Lord of Fire, in the name of thy master, the Lord Michael, Archangel of the Sun!

While you are reciting these words try to imagine the Archangel Michael towering before you, clad as a warrior in shining armour of burnished gold. See the plated kilt and the curved breastplate, the right hand resting upon the runic engraved hilt of the war sword, while the left is concealed behind the round battle shield. His hair streams back from his face like liquid gold and amber eyes like those of some wild jungle beast blaze down from the dazzling countenance of his strong face.

Djinn is a fire giant, as described in the old Norse legends. His lithe body is composed of twisting, living flame and from his slanted eyes sparks crackle and glow. He rises up beside Michael like some demon god from hell, aflame with his own elemental power.

It is safe to assume that neither the Archangel Michael nor his servitor Djinn actually looks like these descriptions but it is considered true that the angelic and elemental spirits appear to the clairvoyant vision in the forms in which man has clothed them. Those descriptions are in fact archetypal images projected by centuries of magicians as their idea of what these astral personages look like.

Ritual for Attracting Money

There are two primary desires which drive people to achieve status in the world' one is money and the other is love. Candle magic caters very well to these desires for there are workings available in its annals which are designed to grant both financial and emotional security.

First, we will look at the material angle. Money may be the root of all evil but many are willing to risk entanglement by attaining this precious commodity. Whether its possession will bring them the happiness they seek is sometimes hard to decide. It usually depends upon their basic character and approach to life. A generous person sharing his last crust with a fellow pauper is hardly likely to become a miser when given unimaginable wealth – or is he?

There are few people in our materialistic society who do not desire money at some time in their life. Even millionaires with money to burn still crave more and more as if terrified that one day all of it will vanish in a puff of devaluation. Although the gaining of financial independence is frowned upon by certain schools of occult thought, there are plenty of occultists willing to risk blasting their souls to attain riches.

Motive is the basic key to what is considered 'right' or 'wrong' in practical occultism. Providing your motive is pure the angels do not mind you having money or gaining it by occult methods, providing you return a small percentage to them by using it to further their work on the earth plane.

Using candle burning to attract money to you means lighting a green candle, which represents abundance and fertility. A purple candle can also be lit to attract good finances and the working should be done on the night of the new moon, the beginning of new things. If possible the sun or moon should be positioned in the sign of Sagittarius, which is ruled by Jupiter, the planet of money luck.

Before doing the spell sit for a few moments clearing your mind of everyday thoughts and impressions. Let your mind open up like a blossoming flower to become a crystal-clear receptacle for the magical power which will shortly flow through it. This silent period of preparation may seem insignificant at the time, but its value will be realized later.

Having lit your candles, five in number, place under each a small coin. In front of the lights position five more coins in the shape of a star.

Some readers will have recognized this symbol already as a pentagram and those familiar with the pack of Tarot cards will further know it as one of the suits of the minor arcana known as 'pentacles'. These are representative of money and wealth in Tarot symbology.

Say: 'Money is a necessary evil and too much

desire for it is an even greater evil. I ... (*insert your name*) desire only enough money for my needs, to accomplish the following ... (*insert your reasons for wanting extra wealth*) and to further the cause of the Great Work.'

Imagine a five-pointed star glowing in purple and green light above the candles. At each tip of this star or pentagram a glittering gold coin reflects the candlelight.

Say: 'Archangel Sachiel! I direct my words to thee that ye may grant my wishes and fill my present need for money. I need this money because ... and not because I am a greedy person who desires to live in luxury above the rank of my fellows. Lord Sachiel, Angel of Good Fortune, grant my wishes and send luck to me.'

Visualize money pouring down in the form of coins from an upturned golden horn. See them spilling down in glittering cascades on to the ground. Imagine this as a horn of plenty which is a bottomless pit of financial accruement.

Sit for a few minutes looking at the flickering candle flame, imagining all the time the money spinning through the ether towards you. Allow the candles to burn out. If need be you can use a Tarot card like The Empress or The Wheel of Fortune – both good luck cards – as meditation symbols during this period.

When this spell works the petitioner may find he has a small win on the football pools or Premium Bonds, or a salary increase. Never imagine that magic produces its results through any other medium than the material plane. Any tyro who expects money to float down from the ceiling after doing a working for money is living in a world of fantasy.

Remember you should always return to the gods a portion of the money received, for 'to give is to receive.' Never mind about how you are going to do this for *they* will find a way. If you fail to honour your side of the contract you may find yourself suddenly faced with unexpected expenses which melt away your winnings. Like faery gold it vanishes back into the astral and will benefit somebody else.

Great fortunes are never made by money spells, so the idle practitioner can not wallow in a despotic life of indulgence. Enough money to cater for your immediate needs is usually the best you can obtain and part of that is returned to the sender as a payment for the sheer audacity of a mortal bothering the gods with such trivia.

Earlier in the book I gave a working for gaining love. Using such spells means that sooner or later the magician will come into contact with the Lords of Karma (fate) who decree that a person must have a certain amount of free will with which to choose their own path. Some occultists do not bother with such details, confident in the self-given knowledge that they are servants of the Karmic Lords, teaching errant souls to experience the richer patterns of life. My own criterion in these matters is that one human being has no right to interfere detrimentally with the life pattern of another or infringe their freedom of self-expression in any way. Anyone who does such a thing is playing with fire, for the Lords of Karma will exact a retribution either in this life or the next which I would cringe in horror from contemplating.

As well as gaining the love of another person one can also ask that you gain the love of everyone. Rather a tall order you might think but magical workings are designed to attract beneficial influences to you and there is no reason why a spell of this type should not be employed to grant happiness.

Ritual for Attracting Love

To attract this happiness to your immediate circle light an orange candle at the time of the new moon. Near the burning candle place the tarot card known as 'The Fool', which in arcane lore represents God in his aspect as the Cosmic Joker.

Say: 'Happiness and love are two hands of the clock of life. My own life which flickers in the emptiness of the world is akin to this candle flame flickering in the darkness.'

Look at 'The Fool' and say:

'I gaze upon the face of the divine fool, the Adept who stands before the abyss of immortality, the babe newly born from the cosmic egg of the Unborn. As I look upon him I see new meanings in my life, new beginnings, new adventures. I see love, happiness and joy flowing towards me. Glory is mine, my cares evaporate like the morning mist and my troubles fall from my shoulders like an unwanted cloak. Life is Love!'

This little working, simple and direct as it is,

will bring new hope into your life and restore your confidence in the power of love to overcome all obstacles and restore all broken dreams.

CHAPTER FIVE

CANDLES FOR SICKNESS AND DEATH

We live in an imperfect world and although tremendous advances have been made we can still see around us fellow men and women who are sick in mind and body. A large amount of time is spent by occultists in healing the sick for it is the unwritten duty of the student of the esoteric sciences to use his knowledge to help others.

Candle burning can play its role in this essential work because there are healing spells which can restore health and vigour to the weak and sick. These workings can either be used by the practitioner to bring comfort to others or to restore his own health in times of need.

Health matters are ruled by the Archangel Raphael, the messenger of the gods known to the ancient Greeks as Hermes, to the Roman emperors as Mercury, to the Egyptians as Tehuti and to the Celts as Merlin. He is accredited by some occultists with the invention of writing, astronomy and the mystical Tarot. Seen in astral vision he wears the garb of a traveller, a yellow cloak and broad-brimmed hat, winged sandals, and carries a staff entwined with serpents which is the ancient symbol of the physician.

As we have seen in our list of colours, red is the one associated with good health. It is the colour of fire which is considered to be representative of the life force and when people are healthy we refer to their 'ruddy complexion', which is considered a sign of vigour. Red candles are therefore burnt for healing, but as health also comes under the rulership of the Lord Raphael, these can be combined with yellow candles.

Try to perform your healing work when Mercury is well aspected in the heavens and if possible when the moon has moved into one of the fire signs of Aries, Leo or Sagittarius. Wednesdays or Sundays are good days for this type of spell for they are ruled by Mercury/Raphael and the Sun/Michael, both of whom can be invoked for healing help.

Ritual for Expurgating Disease

To expurgate disease from a patient's body do your working on the waning moon, for then you can cast away from the physical and astral bodies the conditions which are causing the illness.

Light your prepared, oiled candles and say:

'By the power of these candle flames I draw towards myself (*or insert name of patient*) the healing rays of Raphael. May the blessings of the healing Archangel restore me to full health and vigour.'

Draw the symbol for the planet Mercury on a plain piece of paper. This is an equally-armed Greek cross surmounted by a circle upon which rests the horns of the moon.

Say: 'By this sign I place myself (*or name of patient*) under the cloak of protection of the Lord Raphael. May no dis-ease or illness trouble me and may my recovery to health be sure and fast.'

Place the candles six inches apart and between them imagine in light a wand entwined by two serpents and surmounted by wings.

Say: 'This is the staff of the Archangel Raphael which I send to ... to restore them to health. May its power support and comfort thee in thy time of need.'

You may then blow out the candles.

Colour Guide for Healing

In healing certain colours are traditionally associated with various diseases and their cures. You can, if you wish, use different coloured candles for different ailments. A spectrum scale and its healing qualities are given below.

RED Physical debility; blood troubles; colds; vitamin deficiency.

ORANGE Asthma; fevers; bronchitis and coughs; disability of the bowels; arthritis.

YELLOW Stomach troubles; skin complaints and nervous disorders.

GREEN Heart trouble; high blood-pressure; ulcers and cancers.

BLUE All throat diseases; toothache; headache; headaches and insomnia.

WHITE Can be used to heal any serious disease.

Administering to the Departed

It may seem strange to follow instructions on healing with descriptions of the way candle burning can aid the departed but the fact remains that not all illnesses can be cured by healing. Some are karmic and the person has to die because it has been ordained that he will.

Cases like these do not respond to healing techniques but the healer can assist the soul to pass over peacefully and without pain.

To aid the spirit of the deceased to pass over to the Other Side the practitioner can perform a ritual (which has a certain affinity to the Requiem Mass), to ease the transition from physical to spiritual existence.

White or silver candles should be burnt; and church candles as used on the high altar would be of use here. These are almost pure beeswax and can be obtained from church suppliers at low cost.

Before lighting your candles think of the departed as you last saw them, laughing and happy.

Light the candles and say:

'I light this candle for ... who has passed over from the Earth plane to the Other Side. I remember him as he was in life and I remember his life among his family and friends.'

Pause for a few moments to recollect the deceased's life on earth before his death.

Say: 'I light this candle for ... that he may be taken up in the wings of the dark angel Azrael, Lord of Death. May his soul pass across the Styx to lay in rest in the shining place beyond. May his spirit pass through the portal betwixt this world and the next and find rest and peace. May his time spent in the Land of Light be profitable that he may learn the lessons necessary for his return to Earth and the next stage of his journey towards God.'

Say: 'May ... be at peace and at rest, confident

in the knowledge that his family and friends on the Earth plane are thinking of him and directing their love towards him. Peace be with you.'

Sit silently, allowing the candle to burn down and go out.

Earthbound Spirits

Because of inadequate knowledge relating to death, or fear of dying, some souls resist the process of departing this plane and they become earthbound spirits hovering between this world and the next. If they stay within the surroundings of their earthly environment they become classed as a 'haunting'. In cases like this it may become essential for an experienced occultist to perform a ritual of exorcism. Recent sensational publicity has conjured up an exorcist as a person who wrestles with demons and drives out devils from the possessed. This image is far from the actual truth of the matter, as are many popular conceptions of practical occult work.

For an exorcism white candles again are burnt. If the occultist knows from the results of psychic observation that an earthbound human spirit is responsible for the haunting he can petition the Angel Azrael to collect the wandering soul and guide him to the Other Side. This is one of the tasks of this Angel, who in Ancient Egypt was known as Anubis, the jackal god and 'Opener of the Way' of death.

CHAPTER SIX

CANDLES FOR PROTECTION

A popular subject for discussion among those interested in the occult is psychic attack and, progressing from that topic, 'psychic self-defence'. The latter term is also the title of an occult classic written by the late Dion Fortune (available from Thorsons Publishers Limited), which should be standard reading material for anyone interested in practical magic. Although written in 1935 it is a book containing information of great value pertaining to the harm caused by abuses of psychic power.

Genuine psychic attack is a fairly rare occurrence, although the tyro will meet dozens of people who are being attacked by demons from the lower astral, are suffering from malefic curses, or wilting under the rays of an adept of the 'Left-hand Path'. It all sounds very dangerous and, to the inexperienced beginner, very exciting. In the majority of these cases the alleged 'attack' comes from within and can be more easily cured by psychiatric treatment than any intervention by magical precautions. However, as the old saying says, 'to be forewarned is to be forearmed', and to justify the repeating of that hoary old adage I think it might be prudent to supply you with some magical

ammunition to use against 'things that go bump
on the astral.'

Candles have one big advantage over negative
forces; they are a symbol of light. It is light –
either actual or the metaphorical 'light of
knowledge' – which is the greatest weapon an
occultist possesses in his fight against adverse
powers. In the Ancient Mysteries the candidate's
plea to his initiator was 'from darkness lead me
to light, from the unreal lead me to the real.' The
truth contained in these words should be
engraved upon every occultist's mind for all those
who walk the Path should strive to realize these
ambitions in their quest for the Truth.

As light is an effective antidote to psychic
'nasties', so the best protection is to surround
yourself with a circle of lit candles. Obviously
this is impracticable in the long term but you will
soon discover that psychic attacks come in waves
and not consistently. This is because the attacker
will have neither the time nor energy for a
prolonged onslaught. Using a little occult know-
how, commonsense and observation you will
soon be able to work out the pattern of attack.
These may follow the phases of the moon – which
control so many occult operations – or the social
and business activities of your magical enemy.

The circle of protection mentioned above is a
very powerful device. In esoteric symbolism the
circle represents eternity, which has no
beginning and no end and cannot be disrupted or
destroyed. You are therefore surrounding
yourself by a symbol composed of the most
important and powerful force known to man;

Fire. Within such a circle you should fear nothing for light chases away the shadows, revealing your fears to be empty phantoms.

The Protecting Archangels

While your circle of candles burn, light another candle near you and imagine at the four quarters of the circle four angelic figures. These are the protecting Archangels known as Michael, Raphael, Gabriel and Auriel. Imagine them facing outwards with their hands resting in front of them on the hilts of long swords. If you visualize them in traditional form imagine their huge wings folded back and touching each other at the tips. See the Archangels ringed with golden light and vibrating with power.

Michael is the guardian of the gates of the underworld in ancient mythology and it is to him that you should direct all petitions for help and protection.

'Archangel Michael, Lord of Light! Protect me from the powers of Darkness. Your blazing sword sweeps aside mine enemies, your golden light drives away the goblin shadows. This candle is the symbol of thy light and the light of your angelic brethren before me. By the token of this sign I shall fear no evil this day.'

You should then light a second and third candle to symbolize that your protection has doubled and tripled. Then make the sign of the Greek cross by touching with your fingers your forehead, naval, left shoulder and then right shoulder. As you draw this cross imagine that you are tracing it in pure golden light. This sign is not a Catholic gesture, as some readers may surmise, but the true equal-armed cross used by the magus to seal his aura, for psychic vibrations of a negative type can penetrate the aura.

There are times when negative forces are attracted to certain people and attach themselves to the aura, causing considerable psychic damage. This harm may manifest as dizzy spells, severe headaches, loss of energy and tiredness. Do not get the idea that these are always the symptoms of psychic attack. In many cases they are signs of a medical condition present and a doctor will be of more use than an exorcist. But, in cases where genuine attack is taking place it may be necesary to 'clear' the afflicted victim's aura and candle burning can be utilized to this end.

Blue, silver or gold candles, or a mixture of these, are burnt to attract good influences and dispel negative forces. Again the Archangel Michael is called upon.

'Archangel Michael, here before thee is ... who is troubled by negative powers. It is asked that he should be cleared of this condition and we ask that the negative forces be taken away into the Light. We further ask that ... be cleansed of all astral impurities and that he may attain the purity bestowed by the Angels on the children of Earth.'

As you say these words, visualize rays of blue light pouring on to the affected person and causing the negative forces – which can be pictured as dark blobs in the aura – to break up and vanish. See the person bathed in blue light and looking happy and radiant.

One must not make the mistake of thinking that the acts of preparing, dressing and lighting the candle during operations of this kind are incidental to the words spoken. They are just as important, for the symbolic mime is working on astral levels, the very planes where true magic has the most power. Magic may be performed and realized through physical existence but the real work goes on 'behind the scenes' on the astral plane.

I cannot emphasize too much that candles are focusing agents for the mind and aids to concentration. To disregard the special role of candles during workings of an occult nature is to deprive them of the power to aid your ambitions and grant your wishes.

Candle burning is an ancient art which has endured down the ages because it works. If a type of magic does not work it will be lost from sight because it is of no use to man. Candle burning has never suffered such an ignoble fate and at present a small revival of interest has once again brought it in to prominence.

CHAPTER SEVEN

OPENING THE PSYCHE

Moving away from psychic attack, death and the after life, we are now ready to examine the uses of candles in the attaining and practice of psychic perception.

It has long been the false supposition that only a 'chosen few' have psychic powers and that these are granted to this select elite by the courtesy of God. Like so many 'popular' occult beliefs, this one is totally incorrect for we all contain within ourselves the hidden potential to be psychic.

'Psi' or psychic powers are our common heritage as members of that troublesome and exasperating species known as homo sapiens. Even the psychologist – when not analysing adult mind patterns in terms of infantile breast feeding or lack of it – is beginning, rather reluctantly, to admit that man only uses one-third of his total mind capacity. It is the exploration of the unused two-thirds which occupies occultists, some enlightened scientists, a few psychiatrists, and some doctors who are seeking to discover the Truth.

They believe that at an earlier stage of man's evolution the 'psi' powers were operational but that over thousands of years these 'special' abilities were gradually phased out. Today they lie buried in that two-thirds of the mind we ignore and because of non-use it is difficult for these powers to be liberated.

In a few cases people are born with their 'psi' gifts activated and these rare ones are usually termed 'natural psychics'. Some retain psychic perception during childhood and lose it when they mature but others remain 'psi' orientated all through their life. Others have the psychic potential very close to the surface and with a little training it soon comes out. We all have flashes of 'psi' consciousness during our lives, usually at times of stress or danger, but as the powers are untrained we have no control over them and they come and go. Occult training helps to realize the potential of the powers and also equips us with a moral and ethical background to use as a measuring stick for when we find ourselves facing the dilemma of when to use them to help others.

With candle burning the main use of the candle is for meditation, which means 'planned thinking' or 'contemplation'. It consists of the selection of a certain theme, idea or abstract symbol, viewing it mentally and trying to find out everything about it, observing it from every angle and understanding it. Some books try to tell you that meditation is sitting still, making your mind blank and thinking of nothing in particular. This is partly true but is not the whole picture; meditation is also mental action. To illustrate this point I can tell you that I meditate by pacing up and down a room. Perhaps this is because I think better on my feet but the truth is that ideas and inspiration come to me easily when I'm active. This is true, active meditation.

Clairvoyance and Candle Magic

To train yourself in clairvoyance (from the French 'clear seeing'), which is one aspect of psychism place a candle on the table in front of you. Concentrate on the flame, but do not stare without blinking, for this makes the eyes ache and hinders results. Look at the flame for a few minutes, then look away. Try to clear your mind of all thoughts. This is more difficult than it seems, for the human mind is incapable of remaining in a state of non-thought for more than about 30 seconds without something from another level of consciousness intruding. So take it slowly, in short spasms of concentration-rest, concentration-rest. When you feel tired, rest and try again another time.

Alternatively, the candle flame can be used for clairvoyance by reflecting it into a mirror, crystal or a bowl of water. As romantics realize, candlelight has its own peculiar magic and when reflected on to a polished or mirrored surface it produces very strange effects. It takes on a new meaning and power which create a subtle form of psychic energy sometimes described in old occult books as 'the Astral Light'. In this force field, images and visions can appear.

Clairvoyance using the mirror or crystal is known as 'scrying' and one often hears occultists talk of 'scrying on the astral.' This mysterious phrase refers to visions received via a crystal from the psyche of the seer or from the astral or spirit plane. Scrying is closely connected with the lore of candles and there are many procedures to assist this type of psychic work in the repertoire of candle burning.

Acquisition of psychic powers comes under the rulership of the Archangel Asariel, who is the planetary angel of the planet Neptune, a world associated in ancient mythology with dreams, illusions and the unconscious mind. Asariel is also the ruler of the Zodiacal sign Pisces (19 February-20 March) and one of the characteristics of that sign is the dreamy, mystical state often linked with psychism and its development.

Developing Clairvoyant Powers

If you are interested in developing your clairvoyant powers by means of candle magic, then select a night when the moon is waxing; a few days before full moon is excellent. It is said that the moon tides affect degrees of psychic power and it is true that lunar magic creates the most potent psychic effects when practised by a skilled magus.

Position yourself in a room which is well ventilated. Elaborate robes are not needed. They impress nobody and certainly not the gods, who have seen it all before! Dress sensibly and comfortably and make sure you have plenty of room for movement.

Nine candles should be lit, for nine is the number of the moon. Thirteen is another number associated with the moon (there are thirteen moons to an occult year) and because it was associated with the Old Religion it became an 'unlucky' or 'evil' number. Superstitions such as these usually refer to some obscure or forgotten aspects of the occult art which has been lost to the masses and is only remembered by those who have studied the subject.

At least one of the nine candles should burn on a table in front of you. Behind it should be placed a mirror to reflect the light. Sit looking at the flame, breathing slowly to a 1-2-3 in /4-5-6-7-8 out pattern. Calm the mind, forget all your worries, think only of the work in hand.

Say: 'Angel Asariel! This night as the moon rides high draw aside the Veil which hides the Real from the Unreal. Let me gaze beyond the gates of Malkuth and look upon the astral worlds. Unlock my Third Eye, let me perceive the countenance of the Unknown which is thy kingdom.'

Move the candle to one side and proceed to scry in the mirror. After a few moments the mirror may mist over or coloured lights will be seen floating in it. In some cases bright flashes of light will be seen or whirling patterns traced in fire. These are all signs that your clairvoyance is gradually coming to fruition. Symbols will then be seen in the mirror: faces of human and non-human entities; places and landscapes lit by astral colours; weird mountain ranges illuminated against skies of spectral hue; riders on impossible mounts; futuristic cities with twisting towers rising to twin moons which glide across the night; low boats drifting along mist-shrouded lakes carrying living gods; angels and faeries dancing in woodland groves where stone druid altars lie. The astral plane will give up its secrets to you.

Never scry for too long and fight against the desire to 'lose' yourself in the astral worlds you see. Remember Alice who went through the looking glass? Lewis Carroll knew something of 'secret things' and in his charming fables for the small ones are hidden gems of occult truth. Many investigate the astral, find it more exciting than the earth plane, and become 'prisoners in faerieland'. Do not follow them through the gates of matter, for in this lies madness.

In clairvoyant working, purple candles should be used for they attract psychic influences. Note too that the mirror can also be used for divination and when this is done the seer will be able to discern the omens for the future from the symbols and images which appear in the glass.

For good results with scrying perform the ritual when the moon is placed in the Water trinity; Cancer, Pisces or Scorpio. In practical occultism water is the symbol of 'mind stuff' or the Astral Light which is a carrier of psychic vibrations and magical power.

Many people think that scrying can be accomplished quite easily without the use of candles or calls to the angelic hierarchy. They may well be right but the point is that by using candles and enlisting the aid of the gods the practitioner is strengthening the efficacy of the magic one hundredfold. Therefore he will obtain results quicker and they will be far more potent. If a soldier goes to war it is only sensible to utilize every weapon in his armoury to achieve victory rather then rely on one which may bring about his defeat. It is a wise man who employs all his gifts to fulfil his aims quickly and a fool who wastes energy by only using one at a time.

CHAPTER EIGHT

ANGELS AND CANDLE MAGIC

During this book I have continually referred to the angels and a word of explanation regarding their nature and their link with candle burning might be useful.

We live in a nominally Christian country (even though Christianity in the sense of an organized religion is becoming a minority belief), and because of this our ideas about angels are likely to be limited. Probably we see them as the winged, effeminate young men in night-gowns depicted by some artists and our first reaction is to dismiss these anthropological monstrosities out of hand as the product of fairy tales.

Angelic Guidance

Yet if we take the trouble to read the Bible we find many references to angels who appeared among humanity and guided them with wisdom and knowledge. The best known of these is the Archangel Gabriel who told Mary that she would soon conceive a child who would be known as Jesus. Possibly a less well-known instance of angelic intervention in the affairs of man is the story of the 'Sons of God' who mated with the daughters of humanity and are referred to in the Book of Genesis. Further references to these 'Sons of God' are made in the apocryphal Book of

Enoch, where they are described as 'fallen angels' who taught women the arts of magic, civilization and wisdom.

It is believed that among the gifts given to man by the so-called 'fallen angels' or 'watchers' was the power of fire and candle burning is the utilizing of fire for magical purposes. In ancient Hebrew lore the art of candle magic is placed under the rulership of an angel whose name means 'Lightbearer' and he is in some ways an alternative form of the Archangel Michael.

In reality angelic beings are composed of pure cosmic energy, although usually writers and psychics picture angels in manlike forms, for that is the shape they adopt in their dealings with humanity.

Angels are the 'first created' of God and owe Him a heavy responsibility as teachers. This is why we sometimes refer to 'teaching angels'.

Although there are minor angels, in candle magic we are primarily concerned with the archangels who rule the planets of the solar system; Mercury, Venus, Mars, Jupiter, Saturn, Uranus, Neptune and Pluto. For occult purposes the two 'luminaries' – sun and moon – are considered to be planets, although one is a star and the other a satellite. This makes ten angels but there are two others which make up the mystical twelve; our brief excursion into candle burning has not infringed on their specialist spheres of occult influence.

Surviving Fragment

These angels correspond to the gods of the old

pagan religions and, examining these correspondences, we will soon realize that in reality we are dealing not with many religions but the symbols of *one* religion which is as old as man. This one religion was given to man by the 'gods' or 'angels' many thousands (or even millions) of years ago and the incomplete, fractured, depleted and corrupted natural science we term 'occultism' is the last surviving fragment of that universal teaching of divine origin. In its own small way the art we call 'candle burning' is part of that religion which we sometimes describe as *The Old Religion* to distinguish it from other faiths which are copies of it. In reality every religion invented by man is merely old wine in new bottles and it is to the mystical grape which created the wine that man must now return.

Dark Aspects

One cannot ignore the darker aspects of candle lore, which arose during the time when magic and occultism were shrouded in mystery, superstition and ignorance; a time accurately described as 'the Dark Ages'. In order to dispel the myths concerning these practices I am going to examine some of the aspects and place them in their real perspective against the background of candle magic.

Genuine occultists are generally of the belief that the terms 'white' and 'black' magic are fairly meaningless in practice, although they are applicable in theory. To explain this rather contradictory statement it is necessary to realize that the power used in magic (which originates from the human mind) is a neutral force which can be used for either positive or negative ends. In the final moment the responsibility for the use of the power lies with the magician and depends upon the motive in his heart.

Candles have been used in what the ignorant call 'black magic' on many occasions in the past. Perhaps the most famous instance of their use is the grisly 'Hand of Glory'. This was reputed to be the severed hand of a murderer which was coated in wax and had wicks tied to the fingertips. When lit, this gruesome object had the power to render the occupants of a house unconscious and would open all doors which were locked. Every burglar would be incomplete without one!

Horrific and nonsensical as this seems to our modern view, is there any basis in fact for the grisly item? Yes, but the 'hand' was not a freshly amputated limb from a convicted criminal but an ordinary wax candle in the shape of a hand. Bizarre candles such as these can still be purchased from novelty shops or the amateur can create one worthy of any horror movie by pouring wax into a mould made from a household rubber glove.

Serious occultists would not bother – except as a bit of fun – for it is unlikely that the 'Hand of Glory' would be of any use, even to a cat burglar, and there is no evidence that it can render burglar alarms unusable, so its own usefulness would be limited indeed!

Black Candles
Another myth which needs exploding is the one
about black candles. No paperback 'occult'
thriller is complete without some reference to
candles made of pitch which burn with an
'unholy' blue flame. In genuine practices of
candle burning the colour black is used during
rites connected with the departed and it has no
sinister connotations. Also, as blue is a colour of
spirituality it would seem unlikely that any
'black' magician would burn them in his temple.
Anyway candles made of pitch would create an
odour so unpleasant that the practitioners would
flee the premises choking and spluttering. So
much for black magic.

One usually finds that alleged 'black magic' is
either the product of over-imaginative journalists
or the imaginings of the ignorant who believe
everything and question nothing. Only when the
bright light of reason, logic and intelligence is
cast into the dark places of the mind are the
shadows driven away and the darkness
surrenders its empty secrets.

CHAPTER NINE

THE MYSTICAL NOVENA

It has been said that art imitates life – which limits artistic expression rather savagely – and it could also be said that religion imitates magic. Indeed magic is the elder of the two and in ancient times the chief practitioners of religion were acknowledged as being not merely celebrants of dogma but actual 'priest-magicians'. Therefore we should not be too surprised to discover that one of the most powerful acts of magic that is available to the candle burner also is to be found in a devotion of the Roman Catholic Church. This devotion is called a 'novena' which my dictionary describes as 'special prayers or services enacted on nine successive days'; moreover it is a ceremony shared by both Catholics and ritual magicians. Certainly there is a unity in diversity here!

Concentrated effort is the key to successful magic working, whether with or without candles and other symbolic tools. The novena illustrates this beautifully for it shows the necessity for the person involved to project for a concentrated time his prayers or magical commands, so that 'higher forces' will be stirred into action by his constant repetition of a desired wish. My teacher in magic used an apt example to me once of a man who knocks away at a thick wall with a hammer. As the time passes the wall will slowly crack, split and finally crash down. Magic worked by means of a novena is the same process, hammering away with steady blows till the obstacle is removed.

Non-stop praying sessions, vigils or intercessions are a regular feature of many major religions. In the Christian churches candles are lit to the saints and the faithful kneel in prayer for hours asking that their devotions be rewarded. In the Buddhist temples of Tibet – before the Communist warlords raped that country – a specially designed religious instrument was used for intercessions. This was known as a 'prayer wheel' and consisted of a hollow drum which revolved around a wooden shaft. Attached to the drum was a wooden ball on a length of chain and once set in motion by a spinning action this ball kept the drum revolving with the slightest movement of the wrist. Inside the drum was a tightly wrapped roll of parchment inscribed with hundreds of prayers. Armed with this ingenious 'automatic prayer dispenser' the Tibetan lama could practice his intercession indefinitely with little physical or mental effort involved.

Returning to the West we find that the magician replaces the mortal saints of the Romanist Church with either the non-secular angelic hierarchy or the pagan pantheon of his choice. It hardly matters, except for personal consideration, for they are both symbols of an identical reality clothed in different forms. Saints are mere men in divine raiment but the angels or gods have never been human and never will be.

We have seen how the Catholic prays to his saints and ignores the angels and this leads to another important omission which weakens the traditional power of the novena to produce results. Every hour of the day and night boasts an angelic rulership, which means that a specific angel rules a particular hour, at which time his force is stronger than the rest and the astrological influence of his planet is in some peculiar way 'stronger' than the others in the hierarchy. This does not make much sense from the scientific or rational viewpoint but then the whole subject of magic and indeed of occultism complies with natural laws which operate beyond the spectrum of *known* scientific data. We deal in magic with a 'natural science' which modern physics is close to apprehending.

Individual Rulerships

If one can suspend normal beliefs and accept that this concept of angelic hours is correct in practice, we can pass on to the individual rulerships under the different members of the hierarchy and these are detailed below for the reader's information.

00.00-01.00 hrs	Sachiel
01.00-02.00 hrs	Anael
02.00-03.00 hrs	Auriel
03.00-04.00 hrs	Cassiel
04.00-05.00 hrs	Mikael
05.00-06.00 hrs	Gabriel
06.00-07.00 hrs	Samael
07.00-08.00 hrs	Raphael

08.00-09.00 hrs	Sachiel
09.00-10.00 hrs	Anael
10.00-11.00 hrs	Auriel
11.00-12.00 hrs	Cassiel
12.00-13.00 hrs	Mikael
13.00-14.00 hrs	Gabriel
14.00-15.00 hrs	Samael
15.00-16.00 hrs	Raphael
16.00-17.00 hrs	Sachiel
17.00-18.00 hrs	Anael
18.00-19.00 hrs	Auriel
19.00-20.00 hrs	Cassiel
20.00-21.00 hrs	Mikael
21.00-22.00 hrs	Gabriel
22.00-23.00 hrs	Samael
23.00-24.00 hrs	Raphael

When I was first taught the novena it was shown to me as a turning wheel – a 'Wheel of Fortune' like the tenth card of the Tarot pack – which carries along the vehicle of your desire. It is the wheel of the Chariot (another Tarot sigil) which represents the will as the battering ram used by the mind to achieve its aims.

Each day is truly the first day of the rest of your life, but the day you light the first novena candle is very special for you are setting into motion the juggernaut which will bring about your desires and in using the novena you invoke not one angel – as in the other candle spells given in this manual – but you call upon the mighty angelic host. It is their combined force which unleashes the minor powers sent to bring you the

'luck' or 'good fortune' which will ease the path
to success.

To begin your novena you need a goodly
supply of candles which must be suitable to keep
burning during the long ritual. Night lights or
votary candles are ideal but wicks floating in
small bowls of oil can be used; the bowls should
be made of heavy glass in different colours
representing the planets ruled by the angelic
lords.

Discovering Your Ruling Angel

Before commencing the ritual you must first find
out who your 'ruling angel' is; not your 'guardian
angel', who is somebody quite different, but the
angel ruling the zodiacal sign under which you
were born. Readers in doubt about their ruling
angel can refer to Appendix B of this book, which
deals with *Zodiacal Colours*. Having discovered
your angel you must begin the novena on this day
(this information is given in Appendix A), and on
the exact minute of his hour. This is when you
light your first candle. The novena should end on
his day a week later and is finalized on the last
minute of his hour on that day.

When you do your novena only petition for *one*
wish for it is not designed for a multiplicity of
requests and is not meant to deal with petty
problems. The novena produces results only if
the desire is worthy, for the angels have better
things to do than bother themselves overmuch
with the minute desires of the human race. Also,
do not expect instant results, for like all magic it
takes time for the forces to interplay and the tides

to ebb and flow to produce results. Sometimes it may take up to 28 days (a full moon cycle) for the event to occur, in other times a day and night after the end of the novena sees it done. Remember, our Catholic friends pray for nine days and nine is a number sacred to the moon, who rules all magic.

During the ritual the student must keep the candles burning all the time. Number is not too important. Some people like to have as many candles as angels, which is quite a good idea. Once lit, the candles must be regularly tended and if you are unable to obtain votary lights it is permissible to use candles in rotation; lighting the next set from the old ones but never allowing any to go out. It is a well-known fact that candle flames give off a subtle etheric energy when burning and it is this force field or 'shekinah' which you are striving to tap.

Having lit the candles you must then address your ruling angel:

O Angel ... I light this sacred flame as the first act of my petition to the angelic hierarchy, who it is hoped will look favourably on my request. This light is offered up as a symbol of the inward light illuminating my soul and represents the spark of hope burning in my heart that my petition will be granted.

To illustrate the novena ritual further we will imagine that you wish to pass an important examination upon which the future of your career depends and you would like a little other-worldly help to do this. Say also you are a Leo;

ruled by the Sun and the Archangel Mikael or Michael. This means you will have first invoked him in the preliminary prayer given above. You are now ready to commence the novena. You can either spread the ritual over a week, invoking a different angel on his hour each day, or you can do a 24-hour novena invoking the angels in turn on each hour.

For the sake of argument let us say you are going to be brave and perform the 24-hour rite. You have lit your candles at 04.01 hours on a Sunday. At 07.01 hours on that day you perform the invocation to the Archangel Raphael, who rules the matter under concentration, i.e., the exam results.

> Archangel Raphael, Lord of the Book of Truth, Giver of Laws, Master of the Hidden Word of Maa Kheru, I seek thy help in my time of need. Grant me wise one thy quicksilver powers of mind, thy golden memory and winged pen that I may acquit myself with honour in the coming ordeal. Grant me the faculty of intelligence and understanding that I may triumph.

When the next hour chimes the transfer of rulership to jovial Sachiel you say:

> Archangel Sachiel, angel of this hour, assist me in my coming ordeal and add thy power to that of Raphael this day.

This process is repeated through the day with each angel and at 15.00 hours and 23.00 hours the invocation to Raphael is repeated.

If you cannot face the thought of 24 hours without sleep you can set an alarm clock through the hours of the night in order to wake up when each invocation has to be said. Remember that the candles must be tended and that none should be allowed to go out during the ritual.

CHAPTER TEN

CONTACTING YOUR GUARDIAN ANGEL
– PART 1

Many aspects of candle magic are very ancient indeed and date back to the period of history many thousands, even millions of years ago when men were in direct contact or communication with the Archangels or Gods of the solar system.

This magical period has been remembered by humans in their collective racial subconscious as the so-called Golden Age and is designated in the Judeo-Christian Bible in symbolic terms as the sojourn in the Garden of Eden. The divine garden or earthly paradise is an idealized state of perfection believed by many occult adepts to have existed at the dawn of recorded history when the first humans – referred to as Adam and Eve in the Bible – evolved from their primitive origins and were ensouled with the divine spirit of the Godhead.

During this Golden Age humanity possessed all knowledge, communicated by telepathy with each other and the animal kingdom, and was in spiritual contact with other realms of existence. This is illustrated in an allegorical form by references in The Book of Enoch and Genesis to contact between the Angels and the daughters of men and the fact that the Lord God (Jehovah or

Yahweh) walked among the trees in Eden and talked with Adam.

The Fall from Grace

According to the most ancient and secret occult traditions, humanity misused the esoteric knowledge granted to them and fell into wicked ways. They were symbolically 'tempted' by the serpent of forbidden wisdom (an occult simile for sexual energy) and fell from a state of perfection into 'sin'. This is the Fall described in Genesis when Adam and Eve become aware of their nakedness, don fig leaves to hide their newly formed organs of reproduction and are driven out of the Garden by the angel with the flaming sword, Samuel.

The same story is encapsulated in the myth of the rebellion in Heaven. In that allegory (veiled in Hebrew mythology) the Archangel Lucifer, firstborn of the Godhead, rebels against the divine plan of creation. He is defeated in battle by the Archangel Michael and is banished to assume the title *Rex Mundi* or Lord of the World – a position many occult adepts believe he still holds.

It is after this symbolic battle in Heaven and the Fall from the Garden of Eden that humanity as we know it first came into being as souls incarnated into physical bodies and having the characteristics of the male and female genders. At one stage in our evolution the human race is one with the Gods and at the next we have deviated from the divine plan of Cosmic harmony and fallen from the spiritual plane into gross materialism and the ignorance of worldly matters.

What has this to do with the concept of the Guardian Angel and the secrets of practical occult candle burning? It is significant because through the art of candle magic dedicated students can re-establish communication with the spirit world and make contact with the realm of Angels.

Before explaining the method used to attain the knowledge and conversation of your Guardian Angel I shall digress slightly and explain the difference between the latter and your Ruling Angel.

Your Ruling Angel

In simple terms – for magic, no matter how complicated the self-styled 'experts' may pretend it is, is a simple art – your Ruling Angel is linked with your date of birth and the astrological sign ruling on that day. Look up your Zodiac Sign in Appendix B and make a note of its ruling planet. Then in the list given in Appendix A find the Archangel ruling that planet. Whichever Angel is given is your Ruling Angel.

What does this mean in occult (hidden) terms? It means that you are in sympathy with or tuned in to the vibration of that Angel and his cosmic influence will figure strongly in your life pattern and the lives of all the other people who share your birth sign. When performing the simple rites of candle magic given in this instruction book you can add extra power to them by adding a special reference or petition to your Ruling Angel during their performance.

Petitioning Your Ruling Angel

A suggested petition is given below for guidance. It has been presumed that the candle burner is a Leo (23 July-22 August) and is therefore under the cosmic influence of the mighty Archangel of the Sun, Michael.

> Mighty Archangel Michael, Lord of the Sun and bearer of the holy sword and shield of God, I ... (insert name) call upon thee in my hour of need. Assist me O Michael in the Great Work that I have chosen to do and grant me a successful outcome to my efforts through the divine power of the eternal Lord of Light and Life.

Your Guardian Angel

Your Guardian Angel is rather more personal in nature than your Ruling Angel who, however much you may feel in sympathy with him, must be shared with all the other millions of people in the world who were also born during your astrological birth month. Your Guardian Angel is unique to you and you alone and, in fact, is regarded by some occultists as your own higher self. In folklore and legend an entity of the Guardian Angel type is said to attach itself to a baby at the moment of birth and acts as a protective spirit during its lifetime. This figure is often featured in childrens' fairy tales as the Fairy Godmother character who waves a magical wand over the newborn child and grants it

protection from evil. This guardian spirit may be
one of the spiritual hierarchy called Angels or
Gods or it may possibly be the departed spirit of
an ancestor who returns from the nether regions
to watch over their descendants and keep them
from harm. Similarities between the concept of
the Guardian Angel and the spirit guides which
communicate with Spiritualist mediums are
marked and cannot be dismissed as purely
coincidental.

Belief in Guardian Angels is a very ancient
one. The Romans, for instance, believed in an
entity called a *genius* who not only guarded its
chosen earthly companion but also inspired him
or her with the sacred gifts of the Muses. In
Classical Greece the *genius* was called a *daemon*
(not to be confused with the Christian idea of a
demon or little devil) and was said to haunt
writers, poets and artists, helping them in their
creative work.

The Early Christian Church naturally adopted
the idea of guardian spirits from the pagan
philosophers of Greece and Rome saying that
every man was accompanied by an angel of
righteousness, who inspired his noble actions,
and a dark angel, who led him into temptation
and sin. In the beliefs of the Moslems everyone is
protected by two angels during the day and
another set of two at night. Not only did these
angels protect their charges but they also made
notes on his or her behaviour ready to present
them on Judgement Day when the souls of the
dead were called to task and had to pay for their
indiscretions. Sunset and dawn were the special

times when the guarding angels changed shifts and, according to Islamic lore, these periods were of great danger for the powers of evil could slip under the angelic guard and lay claim to the unprotected soul.

CHAPTER ELEVEN

CONTACTING YOUR GUARDIAN ANGEL
– PART 2

So much for the myths surrounding Guardian Angels, but what of the practical magical techniques used to contact them? In the part of this book which described the clairvoyant art of scrying the use of a mirror to induce psychic vision is mentioned. The mirror again features in the ritual to contact the Guardian Angel. In this case it is a special one and, if at all possible, should be manufactured and used only for the purpose of astral communion with your protecting spirit or higher self.

Making a Magical Mirror
The magical mirror for contacting the Angelic realms should be made when the moon is waxing towards full, on a Wednesday or Thursday, and during one of the hours ruled by the Archangel Raphael (Mercury). The reason for this is that the 'silvering' on mirrors is usually made with mercury or with quicksilver. This is the sacred metal of the planetary sphere of Mercury which is governed by the Lord Raphael.

Very little expertise is needed to make a good magical mirror. It can be manufactured from a round, concave piece of glass. Use a matt black paint to coat the back of the glass (the convex side) and put on several layers applied fairly thickly but evenly over the whole surface. The finished mirror can then be mounted in a square of stiff cardboard or very thin hardboard and placed in an ordinary picture frame – painted or gilted to your design and specification – to make a professional job of it.

Consecrating the Mirror

Before using the mirror in the magical operation of attaining the knowledge and conversation of the Guardian Angel you should *consecrate* it for the task in hand. You do this by putting three teaspoonsful of salt into a small bowl of water while reciting the following words:

> In the name of the Twelve Archangels of the Planets let this water be blessed, purified and psychically cleansed for the Great Work which is in preparation this day.

Eagle-eyed readers will notice that in Appendix A of this book there are only *ten* Archangels listed corresponding to the eight planets in the Solar System (excluding Earth) and the two heavenly bodies of the Sun and the Moon. In fact, this very important ritual also invokes the powers of two more Angels whose attributes and esoteric names are a closely guarded secret among students of the ancient Mystery Schools of the West and are only revealed to initiates. Suffice to say that these extra Angels are linked with the occult teaching that other planets exist beyond the orbit of Pluto, which was only discovered in the 1930s, and that there are also two 'moons' additional to Luna in the vicinity of Earth which are called by occultists Lilith and Vulcan.

Having completed the blessing ritual of the water it is applied to the surface of the mirror with a new cloth or sponge and then it is wiped dry using a separate cloth, which should also have been previously unused, or, as the medieval magician would say, *virgin*.

You are now properly prepared and the mirror is 'charged' ready for you to proceed with the actual magical operation of contacting the Guardian Angel.

Contacting your Guardian Angel

Light one white- or silver-coloured candle in the place you have selected for your work, be it magical temple, study or bedsitter. The number one in numerology is very potent in true magic and evokes powerful influences from the spirit plane. White is an important colour of the spectrum for it not only symbolizes enlightenment of the soul but suggests that the ritual is designed to tune in to the higher levels because of its rare and pure vibration.

As you light the single candle say the following words:

> By the grace of the Twelve Archangels let this place be protected from all harmful influences that may be in the world of phantasms and illusions. Grant the efforts of they humble student in the Great Magical Art be worthy in thy sight O Lords of the Universe and the Stellar Realms beyond the setting Sun.

Place the magical mirror in front of you on a

table or desk so that you can look into it without effort. Turn out the electric lights so the room is only illuminated by the single white candle. Gaze into the mirror as described in Chapter Seven of this book on opening the psyche. Breathe in and out slowly to a regular rhythm and look at the image of yourself reflected back from the mirror. Pretend that the face that you can see looking back at you is that of a stranger, a person you have never seen before. Do not stare without blinking as this can cause eye strain but be relaxed, calm and do not try to hard.

Look if you can *beyond* the image in the mirror. Look *through* the image as if it did not really exist. At this stage in the magical operation you may well become aware of a presence other than yourself in the room. Do not be afraid, it will not harm you – it is only the presence of your *alter ego* that suggests you are beginning to make contact with your Guardian Angel.

Then you may see a flickering light dancing around your head in the mirror. This is the aura and may be in one or more of the astral colours and is another sign that you are communicating with the Angelic realms. As soon as you feel tired cease working for the day and continue at a later time when you are refreshed or on another day when the conditions are right.

Gradually, it may take some time, your efforts will be rewarded. Your image reflected in the mirror may vanish and be replaced by the face of somebody you do not recognize but who seems strangely familiar to you. You will then know that you have truly contacted your Guardian

Angel, spirit guide or higher self (whatever you may wish to call it). He or she (the Angels may appear in female form to men and in male shape to women) might communicate to you by what is termed thought transference or telepathy. That is, the lips of the person in the mirror will not move but you will clearly hear their voice in your mind. Occasionally the voice may speak in the room and others who are present as well as yourself will hear it clearly as if the person speaking was standing next to you and holding a normal conversation.

Also, the spirit companion sometimes calls you by a new name. This is a very special honour and is in fact your *magical name* by which you will be referred to by spiritual entities who contact you from the Other Side. Once you have made contact with your Guardian Angel all manner of teachings and information can be relayed from the spirit world and whole new horizons of spiritual achievement open up before you.

Each time you have finished with your magic mirror it should be wrapped in a length of black silk (not artificial fabric) and put away safely in a drawer or cupboard. On no account should the mirror ever be exposed to sunlight as this can very swiftly neutralize its efficacy.

However, the surface of the mirror does respond well to the rays of the moon, waxing or full, and it can be *charged* or *magnetized* by leaving it exposed to the light of the lunar disc. These same instructions naturally apply equally to any mirrors used in scrying, astral travelling and clairvoyant vision.

CHAPTER TWELVE

CANDLES IN THE MAGIC CIRCLE

Those of my readers who have studied medieval magic will be aware of the importance of the magical circle in the practical operations of the occult path.

Unfortunately, the magicians of the Middle Ages had a taste for the horrific and the sensational and some of the *grimoires* or grammars of medieval sorcery provide some very lurid examples of this genre. One of the worst is the circle described by the famous French nineteenth century magus Eliphas Levi as 'the Goetic circle of black evocations and pacts', which in itself is a pretty chilling description.

In this particular case the melodramatic description was in many ways justified. At the centre of the circle was painted a reversed Christian cross (this had no occult value but it was designed to put the magician into the right frame of mind) which was surmounted by a triple circle representing the three principles of magical working: imagination, concentration and, last but not least, visualization.

Around the circle the magician had to arrange four grisly objects. Namely, the skull of a hanged felon, the severed head of a black tom cat, the horns of a goat that had been fed on human flesh and the corpse of a mummified bat that had drunk human blood.

Normally, the circles used by today's magicians are a lot tamer than this. The circle in practice has a twofold purpose; it acts as a container or storage area for the psychic energy created during the rite and it is also a very useful barrier that prevents the invasion of the working space by negative influences which have no connection with the work in progress and exist only to stir up conditions on the Earth plane.

In occult lore the circle not only surrounds the magician in a two dimensional way (i.e., as a line traced on the ground) but also exists as a three dimensional unit encompassing the magus in a sphere of protection which extends both below and above him. The magician, therefore, has all round cover from every side and angle and a special storage container for the power which is to be generated in the working area during the rituals he or she is to perform within its boundaries.

The Power of Light

What role then does the candle play in the circle? In an earlier chapter we saw how primitive man used fire as a physical weapon to drive away wild animals and as a psychic instrument to protect him from the night demons he imagined haunted the shadows. The use of candles, lamps or torches in the magic circle is an atavistic regression to this ancient belief but one that has been sophisticated and modernized to serve the specialized needs of the occultist of today.

In olden times the shaman or sorcerer would dig a circular trench around his place of magical working, fill it with brushwood and set it alight. This symbolically created a barrier between the shaman and anyone who sought to disturb him during his rituals, it helped set aside the piece of ground he was on as something different or sacred in relation to the surrounding area, and finally it protected him, or so he postulated, from the hordes of evil spirits in the world who would seek to attack him while he was engaged in his occult procedures. This practice survives today in the *circle of protection* described elsewhere in this book as a self-defence against the possibility of psychic warfare.

The Archangels of the Elements

For all other magical workings, excluding psychic self-protection, only four candles set around the circle are deemed to be sufficient (unless some major magical operation such as a Novena is underway) to protect the person who is inside. These candles symbolically represent by their light the presence of the four Archangels of the Elements and the four quarters of the magical circle. They are Michael (Fire), assigned to the south, Raphael (Air), ruling the East, Gabriel (water), guarding the West and Auriel or Uriel (Earth) exercising dominion over the watchtowers of the North quarter.

The *magical image*, or visualization description, of Michael is given in the chapter on spells for love and happiness. Raphael's description is given in the chapter on candles used to cure sickness and to assist the passing of the soul to the spirit world.

Auriel is the dark visaged angel of the Earth element and the planet of Uranus. He usually appears as a rather stern faced man of mature years with flowing silver hair and violet eyes. He also wears a cloak of spectrum hue which rivals Joseph's coat of many colours in the Bible. It literally flashes with astral colours and glowing in his aura, on his forehead and between his eyes, is the famous 'television aerial', which is his planetary sigil or magical seal.

Gabriel is the Angel of the Moon. He appears to clairvoyant vision as a young, strong man with a wise face that shines with inner light. He wears the curved crescent horns of the waxing Moon on his brow, covering the third eye chakra, and is clad in a cloak that reflects like pure mother-of-pearl or crystal glass.

The Kings of the Elemental Kingdoms

Each Archangel of the Elements is accompanied by his personal *magistellus* or elemental servant in the form of one of the mighty Kings of the Elemental Kingdoms. These august presences go by the names of Djinn, king of the Salamanders (Fire), Paralda, the King of the Sylphs (Air), Ghob, King of the Gnomes (Earth), and Niksa, the King of the Undines (Water).

In Egyptian magic and ritual the Elemental Kings are symbolized by the children of the hawk headed god Horus. They are known as Toumathph, represented in the form of a jackal as guardian of Fire, Ameshet, a young man who rules Air, Ahephi, in the form of an ape ruling the element of Earth and Kabexnuf, the commander of the water depths, who is depicted as a hawk. Another representation of the four Elemental Lords is in the Tarot pack where they feature as the Kings of Swords, Wands, Pentacles and Cups.

The traditional magical image of Djinn is given in the chapter of this book on spells for attracting love. The other Kings can be visualized either in their Tarotic or Egyptian forms or in their traditional images as given below.

Paralda is a lithe, writhing figure seemingly made of pale blue mist. His form is tenous and indefinite. Always moving and changing shape as he glides around his master, the Lord Raphael.

Ghob is the King of the Earth and this shows in his solid form. He is squat, heavy and dense. Clairvoyantly he appears, as one would expect, in the traditional image of a gnome or goblin, exuding old age, elemental strength and innate 'heaviness'.

Niksa is the ruler of Water. He is fluid and, like the Air King, ever changing shape. His greenish blue aura flows back and forth, splashed with silver streaks and grey tentacles of power.

If you require a circle to work your candle magic in – and it is not absolutely necessary – it is these Angelic and Elemental Forces that you will be calling upon when you cast the circle before the ritual commences.

Casting the Circle

All circle casting traditionally begins and ends in the East which is traditionally, if not always actually, where the Sun rises each morning. In magical lore the East is the source of vibrations of life, light and power for the Sun represents in occult symbolism the creative principle of the Universe. Because of this the circle is usually drawn in a clockwise – or sunways – direction so that you are flowing with the creative force of the Cosmos and not against it.

The shape of the circle can be cast with a finger, a specially prepared wand or merely with the imagination which is perhaps the most potent magical weapon of all. Whichever way you decide to do it on the physical plane it must always anyway be visualized on the mental and astral levels. You do this by imagining a ring of small flames leaping up where your hand or magical instrument is pointing until you are completely surrounded by a barrier of blue light.

To add extra power and protection to the circle you then call upon the Archangels of the Circle, together with their attendant Elemental Kings, to guard it. You do this in turn, beginning with Raphael in the East and moving around the circle in a clockwise direction using the following words at each quarter:

> Archangel Raphael/Michael/Gabriel/Auriel I ask ye to protect this circle from all negative influences and to show favour to the magical work that I shall accomplish within it this day.

As you call upon each Archangel imagine him in the magical image given to you earlier. It is, of course, foolish to imagine that you, as a mere mortal, are commanding a mighty Angel or God to attend your circle (and in many ways the magical images of the Angels are purely subjective) for if you were to be really exposed to the elemental forces represented by these images you would be blasted into a pile of ash. What in fact is occurring in the circle is that you are tuning in to the vibration of the power behind the Angelic image which is a representation of one of the many aspects of the one Creative Principle.

Closing Down the Circle
When you have completed your candle magic within the circle you then close it down. Again, starting from the point in the Eastern quarter, go around the circle repeating the following words at each compass mark.

> Archangel Raphael/Michael/Gabriel/Auriel your help this day has been welcome and I thank thee for thy protection during this period of my magical work.

The candles around the circle are then pinched out and the magical images of the four Archangels are dissolved. Some students of practical occultism close their circles by walking around them anti-clockwise or *widdershins*, but you may find the candles mysteriously extinguished by an invisible wind if you do this.

This then is the magical circle. No cats heads,

human skulls or other theatrical mumbo jumbo. Like all forms of true magic it is simple, uncomplicated and straightforward.

CHAPTER THIRTEEN

GENERAL SPELLS AND
CANDLE DIVINATION

Although most of the desires of the human mind, heart and spirit are covered in the previous chapters in this book there are miscellaneous candle burning spells which do not fit into any specific category and deserve a separate mention.

The Dream Wish Spell

One of these is the Dream Wish Spell. In our introduction to candle magic the importance of the subconscious mind was stressed together with its receptiveness to images presented to it in visual form. These important characteristics are combined and employed directly by the Dream Wish Spell which is designed to, as it were, catch the subconscious mind off guard, infiltrate it with a projected thought form and thus work a neat and very potent magical trick.

First, you select a candle from your range which is kept exclusively for working magic. Depending on the wish you want to come true a candle of the corresponding astral colour as listed in the earlier chapter on astrological sigils is selected.

Handle the candle – but gently so that it does not break or melt in the warmth of your hands – so that you become tuned in to its special colour vibration. Then, place the candle in a corner of the bedroom so that it is directly opposite to your place of rest.

Light the candle one hour before you are ready to retire for the night and as you do so recite the following words.

Archangel Auriel I look to you for inspiration this night for as I sleep you will do your work in the heavens above, granting the innermost wish that is dear to my heart at this time.

Auriel or Uriel is the angel of the unexpected, the sudden change of circumstances, the unsuspected stroke of luck or, quite literally, as he rules electricity, the 'bolt from the blue'. He is therefore the ideal choice as the patron of the Dream Wish Spell.

Having repeated your invocation to the Archangel of Uranus you must then express your wish in a slightly more concrete form. Take a clean piece of paper (you do not need to worry about making sure it is virgin parchment made from the skin of a young lamb sacrificed at full moon as recommended in the medieval *grimoires* as long as the paper is blank and unused) and with a pencil, crayon or felt tipped pen draw a simple picture of your desire.

Nobody, least of all the Angels, expects you to produce a masterpiece – it is the thought behind the drawing that is all important not whether it is beautifully executed or brilliantly laid out on the paper. It is a visual image used to indoctrinate the subconscious mind into a state where it accepts your art work as a reality and sets into motion the brain waves that will cause to happen what you want to achieve by this spell.

Say you want a new house to replace your present habitat which has a leaking roof, rising damp and an incurable attack of dry rot. On your piece of paper draw the house you really want. Just the outline will do with, say, the number of windows, the front door and perhaps the garden gate in the front.

When you have finished the drawing call once more on Auriel.

> Archangel Uriel, spin the wheel of fortune in my name.
> Grant me this wish that I ask tonight.
> Not for my sake only do I ask this boon,
> but to the greater glory of the Creator who
> is the guiding light in my life.

Take the piece of paper and fold it carefully in three. Then place it under your pillow before you retire for the night. Leave the candle to burn during the hours of darkness — making sure it is amply protected from accidental mishaps because the fire elementals like to play their little games with unsuspecting humans.

In the morning remove the paper from under the pillow and in front of the flickering stub of the candle say the following.

> Archangel Uriel, Lord of Uranus, master of the thunderbolt,
> divine inspirer of men on Earth,
> I thank ye for all thy help in this matter
> and making my wish come true during the night
> hours as I slumbered in my dreams.

The folded paper is then burnt in the candle flame and the ashes disposed of in a safe manner.

During the night, while you have been asleep, the design on the paper has burned into your subconscious mind and events have been shaping on the inner planes to bring about the circumstances that will eventually lead to the fulfillment of your wish.

As stated earlier in this book, if it is a house you want do not expect to receive a telephone call from your local estate agent the very next day offering some grossly inflated sum for your property thus enabling you to purchase the country mansion of your dreams. Neither expect to win £500,000 on the football pools or lottery the following week. Although Auriel does work in dramatic ways the acquisition of material things by magic is seldom easy and corresponds to a complex set of karmic laws. Usually the Angels extract their own levy and in order to keep yourself in their favour you may find yourself paying back to them a percentage of your magical winnings. Naturally, this will not be a quarterly tribute in gold coin paid by a dusky maiden but the Angels have their own ways and means whereby you do their work – without ever realizing it – on the Earth.

Astral Travel

A variation on the Dream Spell can also be used for astral travel. In occult tradition the physical body has an etheric or astral counterpart which can leave its fleshy habitat and travel at the speed of light to explore all the corners of the world and journey to other planes of existence to experience the wonders of the spirit realms.

Again, light your candle as in the Dream Wish Spell but this time address your invocation to the Archangel Asariel, ruler of the mysterious, misty planet of Neptune, who has rulership over the psychic worlds and the astral plane.

Lord Asariel, ruler of the astral realms
beyond the stars of heaven,
show me in my dreams the place I wish to
visit in my astral body.

Write on a piece of clean, blank paper the place you wish to visit or the person you want to see in your astral travels and place it beneath the pillow on your bed. It is a sure thing that you will dream about what is written on the paper during the night.

Telling the Future

A candle can also be used as a *magistellus* or familiar spirit and can be trained to tell the future. This may seem a rather strange statement to make but personal experience proves it to be correct. Select a new candle which has not previously been lit. Anoint it with oil as described earlier in the book. Then, say the following words.

Candle, candle, sign of Light,
in the name of the Archangels,
I conjure thee to be my magistellus.

Candle, candle, tall and strong,
in the name of the Life Force within me,
I command thee to be my guide and servant.

Candle, candle, ray of light,
in the name of the Ancient Ones,
I instruct thee to obey my commands
and show me secrets, past and future,
present too.

Light the candle and place it on a table or desk in front of you. Stare intently at the candle flame (to alleviate strain, blink the eyes at regular intervals) and *will* it to rise and fall. You may if you wish use your hand to draw the flame up and down for it will respond to the auric vibrations emanating from your palm and fingers. After some practice you will be able to command the candle flame to rise and fall as you wish and you will have proved your mastery over the fire genii who inhabits the light of the candle's flame.

Having done this you can instruct the genii to predict the future for you or give advice on problems. This is done quite simply by means of a question and answer session using the rising up of the candle flame to signify a 'Yes' response and the waning of the flame to mean a 'No' to your posed query or problem. In fact, as the more astute of my readers will have realized by this stage, you are communicating with your own subconscious mind via the candle genii or spirit and using it to answer your questions and problems. This is a similar process to most forms of divination including the tarot cards, I Ching yarrow sticks, Rune stones, ouija boards or the progressions of the astrological horoscope.

Candle magic is virtually a limitless (except by the scope of your own ingenuity) occult art and can be employed in most spheres of life to ease it along. A candle placed next to a box of seeds or young plants, and accompanied by a sincere petition to Michael, Gabriel and Anael (or all three) usually assures that they will grow strong and healthy.

Weather Making

Occult candle burning can also be used for weather making as in the following little spell.

On a cloudy day place a new candle on the windowsill – away from the curtains of course! – and light it saying the following.

> O Angel of the Morning,
> Lord of the Golden Dawn,
> hear my petition.
> Sweep back these grey clouds of gloom,
> which gather in the heavens above.
> As this tiny light shines below,
> so let the shining Sun blaze above
> to awaken all the forces of Nature
> and bless all living creatures with
> its rays of glory.

As stated in Chapter One, the use of the Archangelic magical images is employed to simplify matters and is in accordance with the fact that most people in the Western world are educated and brought up as Christians, whether or not these beliefs persist in maturity is not important, for the images implanted into the mind at a tender age are those that tend to persist long after the person has passed into adulthood. Therefore, the concept of Angels is a well known one to the majority of people who are reading this book and are probably newcomers to the occult path or practical magical techniques.

However, those who follow non-Christian religious or magical traditions (and in our changing, evolving society their numbers are on the increase) can substitute their own names for those of the Angels.

Alternatively, they can call upon Thoth, Isis, Hermes, Pan or any of the classical Greek, Roman, Egyptian, Saxon, Norse or Celtic pantheon of gods and goddesses who take their fancy. The names are not important for, as the famous English occultist and writer Dion Fortune said, 'All the Gods are but one God.'

CHAPTER FOURTEEN

SOME CONCLUSIONS

In this short introduction to the practical art of occult candle burning we have examined the use of magic, i.e., unliberated mind power, to create certain effects; to heal, to attract good fortune and luck, to achieve financial security, to protect, to win love, to help the practitioner in many ways.

Eight Fundamental Rules

I hope that the basic tenets of candle magic have been easily understood by my readership but the main points can be clarified as follows:

1. Candles are used to create 'magical' effects because they focus concentration and attract certain types of influences. Candle burning puts the magician in the correct state of mind for the easy accomplishment of his aims.

2. Different colours have different vibrations and oscillate psychically on different levels. Every colour attracts different influences and the magician must choose the correctly coloured candle to suit the purpose of the working.

3. A candle may be used to represent any third person by using a candle coloured in the hue of the zodiacal sign of that person. The colour is chosen by knowing the person's

birthdate and then referring to the table in the Appendix of this book.

4. Movement of an influence or desire towards or away from a person can be symbolized by moving the coloured candles. In this way you are affirming Shakespeare's assertion that 'All the world's a stage, And all the men and women merely players'. In this way the altar or table on which you place the candles becomes a chessboard representing the conditions of your life.

5. Candles used for an act of magic should *never* be used again but allowed to burn down. In all cases brand new or *virgin* candles should be used. If possible make your own. If you have to buy them from a shop never haggle over the price and always give the *exact* money for them.

6. Always 'dress' or oil a candle before using it, for this simple act magnetizes it and imparts your own vibrations into it. You and the candle become one.

7. Never use candle burning to influence people against their will or to bring about harm to anyone. Like all magic power, if misused it can turn against you.

8. Always take notice of the cosmic tides which are controlled by the sun and the moon. Try and work *with* these tides, for to try to fight against them is hard, unnecessary work. Remember, attract on the waxing moon and banish on the waning moon. Never work in the 'dark of the moon' (three days before new moon); and remember that full moon is good for spells concerning the gain of psychic prowess.

These eight rules are fundamental to candle burning. Using them the reader should be able to produce the desired results with little practice. Once he has worked out his *modus operandi* he can make up his own workings using the basic outlines given in this book for his guidance.

Always remember that all you will get out of magic depends entirely on what you put in. People who know little about practical magic think all you do is dress up, mumble 'words of power', wave a magic wand; and that miracles will follow shortly. Such nonsense is for a children's fairytale and has no validity in fact. Magic is hard work, yet it is also simplicity itself. Many people feel exhausted after doing a working and that is because they have put their whole being into the act, which is how it should be.

Only by achieving mastery over Fate can you become a Master of your own destiny. In its simple way practical candle burning is the first step on that path and although classified as 'low' magic it is a stepping-stone to the high magical art.

APPENDIX A

THE ANGELIC HIERARCHY

In this book we have seen how each aspect of human life is ruled by a different planetary angel or Elohim. Listed below are the angels, the planets they rule and their spheres of influence.

MICHAEL Archangel of the Sun. Rules all matters of ambition, career and personal finance. Day: Sunday.

RAPHAEL Archangel of Mercury. Rules writing, intellectual ability and healing. Day: Wednesday.

ANAEL Archangel of Venus. Rules love, marriage and anything connected with art, beauty and music. Day: Friday.

GABRIEL Archangel of the Moon. Rules all matters connected with women, conception and natural clairvoyance. Day: Monday.

SAMUEL Archangel of Mars. Rules anything to do with machinery, grants courage and protects from dangers leading from fire or violence.

SACHIEL Archangel of Jupiter. Rules the gain of money, prestige or social eminence. Also gambling and games of chance. Day: Thursday.

CASSIEL Archangel of Saturn. Rules property matters. Anything to do with land or houses. Affects old people, karmic matters and the destiny of the human race. Day: Saturday.

URIEL Archangel of Uranus. Has rulership over magical forces, sudden changes, astrology and anything to do with inspirational matters.

ASARIEL Archangel of Neptune. Rules clairvoyance, matters connected with the sea and the hidden side of life.

AZRAEL Archangel of Pluto. Rules death, the after-life and matters relating to buried treasure or gems mined from the earth.

APPENDIX B

ZODIACAL COLOURS

Each sign of the Zodiac has its own colours and although there may be slight differences between various schools of thought, the generally accepted versions are as follows:

ARIES (21 March-20 April) Ruling Planet: Mars. Shades of red, usually the darker hues of scarlet or crimson.

TAURUS (21 April-21 May) Ruling Planet: Venus. Green, ranging from the palest apple greens to the dark olive of the Earth forces.

GEMINI (22 May-21 June) Ruling Planet: Mercury. Yellow is the colour for this sign.

CANCER (22 June-22 July) Ruling Planet: the Moon. Pale blue and silver are the colours of the Crab.

LEO (23 July-23 August) Ruling Planet: The Sun. Gold, orange, and sometimes red.

VIRGO (24 August-23 September) Ruling Planet: Mercury. Rich browns of the newly tilled earth and the russet hues of autumn leaves dying in the wind.

LIBRA (24 September-23 October) Ruling Planet: Venus. Royal blue and rose pink.

SCORPIO (24 October-22 November) Ruling Planet: Pluto. Black, silvery grey and dark red.

SAGITTARIUS (23 November-21 December) Ruling Planet: Jupiter. Purple and dark blue.

CAPRICORN (22 December-20 January) Ruling Plant: Saturn. Dark brown, greys and black.
AQUARIUS (21 January-19 February) Ruling Plant: Uranus. All colours of the spectrum.
PISCES (20 February-20 March) Ruling Planet: Neptune. Sea green and mauve.

When these zodiacal colours are used in conjunction with the angels and their planetary rulerships, the student can work out a complete system of correspondences for application in practical candle burning.

Good luck!

INDEX